Dear Georgia,

Dear Georgia,

by Beulah Fern Stevens

Southern Publishing Association
Nashville, Tennessee

This book was
Edited by Richard Coffen
Designed by Robert Wright

Type set: 9/11 Optima

Printed in U.S.A.

Library of Congress Cataloging in Publication Data

Stevens, Beulah Fern, 1937-
  Dear Georgia . . .

  1. Christian life—1960-   2. Stevens,
Beulah Fern, 1937-   I. Title.
BV4501.2.S758   248'.4   78-13546
ISBN 0-8127-0204-2

I looked at the clock at the back of the classroom. Twelve o'clock—time to dismiss. "If there are no other questions, that will be all for today." Students closed their notebooks and began to gather books, sweaters, and purses. I picked up my lecture notes and prepared to erase the blackboard. Several students came to the front of the room: one for an adviser's signature to increase his class load, one to clarify part of the next week's assignment, some for other attention. But the one that stands out in my mind is Georgia.

"Beulah," she said, "Katie Day and I want to memorize texts. Do you have some you would recommend? We get together each Tuesday to study the Bible."

"Oh, my," I said, "there are so many."

Georgia just kept looking at me expectantly. I don't know what elicited my initial response. Perhaps it was the six or more other students gathered around the desk, each needing attention. Perhaps it was the magnitude of trying to decide which of many marvelous texts to share. Nevertheless, as Georgia waited, I knew I could not disappoint her. I had watched both Georgia and Katie grow as they had progressed through the nursing curriculum.

The two girls came from different religious backgrounds, and both had religious persuasions different from my own. Nevertheless, I admired their Christlike dedication and characters. They, like some others of their classmates, had chosen this particular nursing school because of its Christian philosophy. No, I would not disappoint them.

And so, as quickly as I had said, "Oh, my, there are so many," I added, "but there are some that are special to me. I'd be glad to share them."

"Would you?" Georgia smiled gratefully. She glanced around at the waiting students. "You don't have time right now," she commented as she handed me a blank piece of paper. "If you'll just write them down here, you could give them to me at the hospital tomorrow."

Georgia's request inspired the thinking that went into this book. Therefore I have addressed it to Georgia, a nursing student. However, the pages that follow are dedicated to all Christians who want the Word of God written in their hearts and manifested through living action in their lives.

Dear Georgia,

Yesterday you asked me to recommend some texts to you. You said that each Tuesday you and Katie get together to memorize passages from the Bible. Before I share some that are special to me, I'd like to share part of my underlying philosophy.

God longs to communicate with us. Because He wants us to discern His messages of love and hope, He has carefully preserved His Word through the ages. In the beginning He walked with Adam and Eve on a daily basis. He talked with them face-to-face. Then the Fall came. Man could no longer have such intimate communication with his Maker. But that did not mean God no longer loved man. No, far from it. In fact, He had already planned a way to restore man to Himself. As you know, that plan involved God the Son coming to live among men and paying for their sins with His own life on Calvary.

That plan also included God, the Holy Spirit, who would inspire men to record His promises and guidelines for living. It included the preservation of these in what we call the Holy Bible. It fascinates me that though over 1500 years passed between the time Moses first wrote the Genesis story until John wrote Revelation from Patmos Island, I find that every precept in the Bible is congruent with all the others there. This in itself is to me valuable evidence on which to place my trust.

When the apostle Paul wrote to the Corinthians, he told them that spiritual things "are spiritually discerned" (1 Corinthians 2:14). I have found much added blessing and understanding when I invite the Holy Spirit to sharpen my mind as I read from God's Word.

Then, as I read I try to consciously visualize the words and passages, and it helps me comprehend the meaning and insight God has for me. It also gives a basis on which to memorize certain passages. I would urge you to try this too.

In addition, I find that God speaks to me through the experiences of life. I'm sure He does the same for you. I find it helpful to keep a diary of special promises and principles as I have seen them demonstrated in my own living. Perhaps you would like to develop a notebook or some other means of keeping record of the texts you memorize and of the application you see in your life.

I commend you and Katie on the project you have undertaken. I know God will bless you immeasurably as you seek to write His precepts on your heart and in your mind.

Promises From the Psalms

Whether I am joyful or sorrowful, encouraged or discouraged, elated or distressed, it seems like David wrote a psalm that just fits. I think I have used Psalms more than any other book for my own comfort as well as to share with others. I will include some of the passages with special meaning for me. No doubt you can add many more to the list.

Psalm 37:39. "But the salvation of the righteous is of the Lord: he is their strength in the time of trouble."

This text fits many situations. It does not promise that just because we have given our hearts and lives to God, we will no longer have trouble. No, far from it. We live in the land of the enemy. We know that one day the enemy will be silenced forever. However, at the present he still is doing all the harm he can.

If God protected us from trouble just because we had chosen Him, we would be in danger of serving Him simply for an insurance policy. We would not have the privilege of demonstrating to the universe that we serve Him because we love Him—no matter what. But here comes the important part—does He leave us alone in trouble? Indeed not. The psalmist said, "He is their strength in the time of trouble." Praise the Lord! What more could we ask? With that kind of help, how can we fail?

Psalm 23. "The Lord is my shepherd; I shall not want. He maketh me to lie down in green pastures: he leadeth me beside the still waters. He restoreth my soul: he leadeth me in the paths of righteousness for his name's sake. Yea, though I walk through the valley of the shadow of death, I will fear no evil: for thou art with me; thy rod and thy staff they comfort me. Thou preparest a table before me in the presence of mine enemies: thou anointest my head with oil; my cup runneth over. Surely goodness and mercy shall follow me all the days of my life: and I will dwell in the house of the Lord for ever."

Many times patients who have been only nominal Christians until they face severe illness find hope and comfort in this passage. The Shepherd Psalm is so widely known that even though their lives have not consciously centered on Christ, they have a certain familiarity with the promises here.

Mr. K. was like that. Not only had he been active but also daring through his forty-six years. Then, quite suddenly, he experienced the acute pain of arthritis. From his hospital bed he shared with me his frustration and fears: "I'm not going to live with this kind of pain! I told my wife last night that I will commit suicide first."

We talked about the pain, the frustration, the prognosis of a crippling disease. We talked about ways of working with the pain. We talked about dependence on

God. And then he began to quote, "Yea, though I walk through the valley of the shadow of death. . . ." He had a hope. He could endure.

Psalm 34:9, 10. "O fear the Lord, ye his saints: for there is no want to them that fear him. The young lions do lack, and suffer hunger: but they that seek the Lord shall not want *any good thing*."

Having been single myself for many years, I understand many of the problems and frustrations of the Christian who lives alone. Since my marriage to a God-fearing man whom I love and appreciate, I have a continued interest in the welfare of the single person and have spent considerable time talking with single women friends.

Wilma—one such friend—described her feelings of loneliness. She related that sometimes she felt rejected and unloved. But through it all, she held fast to this one promise: "But they that seek the Lord shall not want any good thing."

Today Wilma, happily married, rejoices that God helped her wait until she met just the right person. Even so, she trusted the Lord to provide for her the "good things" of life—to fill the loneliness and drive away the rejection, though she knew it was possible she might never marry. God's hand is not limited. He can provide for our basic needs in ways we could not begin to imagine. Our part is to trust Him.

Psalm 34:4. "I sought the Lord, and he heard me, and delivered me from all my fears."

My mother shares a beautiful testimony that makes

Psalm 34:4 meaningful to me. At seventy-one years of age she learned that she needed major surgery. One of her biggest fears was that she would be afraid.

Living by herself in the farmhouse where she had reared her four children, she had plenty of time to reflect on the potential risks of the upcoming operation. However, instead of dwelling on the fears, she studied God's Word, claimed His promises, and committed everything to Him. Here are her words: "When the day came for my surgery, I had absolutely no fears or uneasiness. As my stretcher was wheeled into the surgery and I was placed on the operating table, I had no fears. . . . Following surgery I had almost no medications for pain or distress of any kind. By the third day I was walking the full length of those long corridors. . . . By the end of the second week I was out, driving my own car and getting around as if nothing had ever happened to me. Truly, I feel that the Lord did a miracle for me."

The doctor remarked to my brother after the surgery, "She's a pretty tough ole gal." Her children knew she was a woman of great faith. God had indeed delivered her from fears.

Psalm 34:13, 14. "Keep thy tongue from evil, and thy lips from speaking guile. Depart from evil, and do good; seek peace, and pursue it."

If you examine the promises of the Bible closely, you will find repeatedly that the promise is accompanied by directions to the receiver regarding his part in gaining possession of the blessings. God does not force His gifts on us. We must be willing to receive them. To do this we must cooperate with the guidelines He provides.

Psalm 34 admonishes us to keep from speaking deceitfully and to concentrate on doing good deeds. This does not mean we earn the blessings. It means we are opening the channels through which God can work. If we ever develop Christlike characters, we must learn to control our words. By ourselves it is a hopeless task. With God's help, we can do anything. I need Him to help me in this area. How about you?

Psalm 35:1-3. "Plead my cause, O Lord, with them that strive with me: fight against them that fight against me. Take hold of shield and buckler, and stand up for mine help. Draw out also the spear, and stop the way against them that persecute me: say unto my soul, I am thy salvation."

I first discovered this psalm a few years ago when I felt deeply distressed over an office situation. I recognized intellectually that the accusations against me resulted from an unhealthy organizational position, not my lack of integrity. Yet, emotionally, I carried a very heavy burden. I searched my mind and heart to root out any evil motive that might be contributing to the problem. I searched the Scriptures for guidance.

Miraculously the Lord led me to Psalm 35. With God as my defense, why should I worry? I could freely carry on His work in a normal manner. I need not spend time playing games of attack and counterattack.

Since that original experience with Psalm 35, I have

turned to it on several occasions. Sometimes in my human efforts to solve problems I have not resorted to it as soon as I needed to, but I've noticed that each time I step back and let God serve as my defense, the problems seem to be resolved.

Psalm 91:11, 12. "For he shall give his angels charge over thee, to keep thee in all thy ways. They shall bear thee up in their hands, lest thou dash thy foot against a stone."

Living on a small farm in central Washington, for many years my "world" was about a fifteen-mile radius. At times we would watch the white streams across the azure sky made by airplanes speeding across the continent. Never do I remember identifying with those airplanes. I do not remember ever even fantasizing that someday I might fly in one.

Since that time I have flown many times. As the jet engines roar and the captain announces the takeoff, I always wonder at the power it takes to lift that machine and its cargo off the ground and into the air.

The plane, rushing down the runway, gains speed and finally lifts into the air. The force of its power pushes me back into my seat. Without fail the phrase "They shall bear thee up in their hands" goes through my mind, and I thank God for His angels.

Psalm 34:7. "The angel of the Lord encampeth round about them that fear him, and delivereth them."

The pastor had preached an especially thought-provoking sermon about angels. He had suggested that an angel remains by our side at all times. In fact, he had mentioned that sometimes he talks to his angel. That had impressed me because I, too, have thought about talking with my angel but wondered if I was silly.

All this had occurred two days before in church. Today I was on the freeway driving toward Loma Linda, where I would meet my students for practice at the Medical Center. I was thinking of each student, praying to meet his needs for that day, planning approaches I would take. Suddenly the driver in the car just ahead and to my right swerved toward the lane I was using. For one fleeting moment it seemed I froze. I could see the cars coming together. In my imagination I heard the crash of metal. I knew they would collide.

Although the morning traffic was heavy, I saw no one to my immediate left. I braked and swerved left. At the same instant the driver of the other car realized that she was changing lanes without looking and swerved back into her lane. We went on down the freeway. For the next few miles I reflected on the incident. "That was a close call," I mused. Then suddenly the thought leaped into my mind, "My angel!" "The angel of the Lord encampeth round about them that fear him, and delivereth them."

Psalm 68:20. "He that is our God is the God of salvation; and unto God the Lord belong the issues from death."

When we talk of God's protection and guidance, we would be deluding ourselves if we did not face the fact that sooner or later Christians and non-Christians do die on this earth. Until Christ comes again and reestablishes His kingdom, until the work of the evil one is ruled out forever, Christians as well as non-Christians will experience death through accident and disease. I do not consider death a normal process of life, for it is not as God originally designed. However, the Christian need not lose his faith in God's ever-guiding hand. When faced with sorrow from loss of a loved one, he can feel confident that even more important than life on this earth is the promise of salvation.

Promises From
the Old and New Testaments

James 1:5. "If any of you lack wisdom, let him ask of God, that giveth to all men liberally, and upbraideth not; and it shall be given him."

Georgia, I know you've done much planning and praying about what you should do after graduation. You face such questions as where you should work, whom you should marry, and what God would have you do. I know you have deep faith in God's leading and are open to His direction. Here is a promise you can claim for making decisions in any one of those important areas.

I've found this verse especially helpful not only in the big decisions of life but also in the lesser ones. God does not promise to cover negligent deficiencies, but through study, experience, circumstances, and the Holy Spirit's leading wisdom comes. You can count on that.

Hebrews 10:38. "Now the just shall live by faith: but if any man draw back, my soul shall have no pleasure in him."

All my life I wanted to be a nurse, and never have I experienced a more glorious moment than that summer night in Portland, Oregon, when the dean of the school of nursing pinned the coveted cap on my head. I had visions of being a caring "angel of mercy." Little did I realize how many years I would spend planning and organizing, counseling and studying, to help others administer the tender loving care. In that process my own nursing skills rusted, and I felt awkward in actual practice.

Finally, the time came that I began to see a possibility for getting more directly involved with patients again. One part of me said, "Great! Get going." Another part of me felt hesitant and fearful. During that time I read this text: "Now the just shall live by faith." It was very familiar to me, as it is to many Christians. After all, it's the text that inspired Martin Luther and brought rocking changes to the Christian world. However, that last part—"but if any man draw back, my soul shall have no pleasure in him"—I had never particularly noticed before. It seemed to provide the answer. I would hesitate no longer. I would move ahead in faith.

John 15:5. "Without me ye can do nothing."

Philippians 4:13. "I can do all things through Christ which strengtheneth me."

These verses make good companion texts. John recorded Jesus' reminder that without His power we are really quite helpless. The apostle Paul reminded us that with Christ's strength we can do anything.

These texts became especially meaningful to me after I attended a workshop a few weeks ago. During one of the small group discussions, a kindly appearing, seemingly successful businessman shared the fact that until four years before he had been "hopeless." Then he found

God. Since that time, God had completely changed his life.

The following day I had an opportunity to talk with Ken in more depth. "I sensed when you were talking in our group yesterday that you enjoy a deep religious experience," I told him. "I'd be interested in knowing more about it." What followed was a beautiful description of how Ken had found God. Then he paused. His eyes narrowed. He shifted his weight from one foot to the other. "But you know," he confided, "I still have a problem. I'm critical of people."

"Well, yes," I replied, thinking of my own struggles in this area. "I think we all have that kind of problem."

"Yes," he responded, "but you know, the people in my church really get to me sometimes. They keep saying they're nobody. They're right. By themselves they *are* nobody, but through Christ we can do everything. God expects us to do big things. We shouldn't all the time belittle ourselves." Then he added thoughtfully, "I may have to find another church."

Georgia, I gained a deep insight that day. And I commend to you the promise, "I can do all things through Christ which strengtheneth me." But without Him we "can do nothing."

Romans 12:2. "And be not conformed to this world: but be ye transformed by the renewing of your mind, that ye may prove what is that good, and acceptable, and perfect, will of God."

When this text started penetrating my consciousness, I

began to experience a new freedom in living. Throughout my life I have carried an especially heavy burden in needing to feel accepted—needing to belong. I don't like being different! I suspect you have experienced the same kind of feelings, and no doubt you can easily identify with these needs. Every human being feels them to one degree or another. However, for those of us who tend to have an extra measure of these needs, this text is very special.

Take a look at it again. "Be not conformed to this world: . . . be ye transformed by the renewing of your mind. . . ." God has a plan for each of us. We do not have to conform to the world around us. Each has the freedom to be transformed into the unique individual God designs him to be. How exciting! Surely such a realization should motivate us to study God's Word carefully and to be closely tuned to His leading. May God bless you, Georgia, as you continue to grow into being the very special person God has planned.

Joshua 1:9. "Have not I commanded thee? Be strong and of a good courage; be not afraid, neither be thou dismayed: for the Lord thy God is with thee whithersoever thou goest."

Joshua 1:9 has meant much to me for many years. As a senior in high school, I decided to read my Bible from Genesis to Revelation. I had just finished reading about Moses: his life, his trials, his victories, and his death. And now, in the first chapter of Joshua, I had begun to read the Lord's conversations with the man whom He had chosen to assume the leadership for that great multitude of people. Notice that three times in the first nine verses the Lord commands Joshua to be strong and of good courage. By the third command it seemed to me that the words fairly leaped from the page into my consciousness. They have carried me through many ensuing years and times.

Careful reflection on the first nine verses of Joshua reveals interesting insights. Besides having commanded Joshua to be strong and courageous, besides having promised His ever nearness, God laid out the conditions that would make Joshua and the people open to receive the promises. Notice verse 7: "Only be thou strong and very courageous, that thou mayest observe to do according to all the law, which Moses my servant commanded thee: turn not from it to the right hand or to the left, that thou mayest prosper whithersoever thou goest."

There Joshua had it: not only the promise but also directions to follow. A fascinating study in God's Word demonstrates that with the promises He reveals the conditions under which we can best be open to receive them. I would challenge you to search for the directions that come with the promises. I can assure you that your life will be fuller, richer, and more abundant.

Isaiah 41:13. "For I the Lord thy God will hold thy right hand, saying unto thee, Fear not; I will help thee."

My friend Ruth first brought the verse to my attention. We had been working together on some especially difficult administrative problems in the nursing department. One day she stopped by my office. "Someone showed me this text," she pointed out. "I want to share it with you."

It's a beautiful promise. Can't you just imagine God's strong hand reaching down from heaven as He says, "Don't be afraid. I'm here, and I have everything under control"?

I don't know about you, Georgia, but I am right-handed. If God holds my right hand, I can do very little without Him. Perhaps you are right-handed, too, but I suspect that if you are left-handed God would just as willingly hold that one. When we give Him the predominant role in our lives, we can say with Paul, "If God be for us, who can be against us?" (Romans 8:31).

1 Timothy 6:15. "God . . . is the blessed controller of all things" (Phillips). Usually I prefer memorizing from the King James Version of the Scriptures. Perhaps it is because I am more familiar with it. Perhaps the older English style captures my attention better. Nevertheless, occasionally I have a special appreciation for some of the newer translations. Phillips' translation of 1 Timothy 6:15 is a good example.

Since I've learned to commit everything to God, it has taken much of the stress and strain out of daily living. Oh, yes, there are still problems. Sometimes it takes me a while to work my thinking process around to really apply this message that Paul shared with his young friend Timothy. It amazes me, however, how many times when someone is late or my car breaks down or I have to attend an unexpected committee meeting, or whatever the distraction may be, these words come to my rescue. Write them on your heart and in your mind, and then actually say them aloud next time you encounter distraction. I predict that you will be amazed, too.

Matthew 5:16. "Let your light so shine before men, that they may see your good works, and glorify your Father which is in heaven."

This past quarter a small group of nursing students has met each week to seek meaningful and appropriate ways of providing spiritual support to patients. God made it my privilege to be the faculty member studying with them. In our study we probed ways of identifying felt spiritual needs, ways of approaching the subject, ways of suggesting Christ to those who do not know Him. Through the study this text, "Let your light so shine, . . ." took on new meaning for us.

We noted that Jesus did not say, "*Make* your light so shine." He said, "Let" it shine. Letting it shine meant to us considering each interaction with someone as a divine appointment—one in which we have the opportunity to affirm someone with whom God has brought us in contact. It meant depending on the Holy Spirit to guide our words. It meant not forcing the issue.

Letting it shine meant following the admonition Jesus had given just prior to this statement. While on the one hand we do not make the light shine, on the other hand we do not hide it under a basket. We must take advantage of each opportunity to share our hope in Jesus. We even study and practice to be adept in our skills in sharing. But we depend on God to give us the right thoughts. When we do this, we can rest confident that our Father in heaven will be glorified.

Matthew 5:9. "Blessed are the peacemakers: for they shall be called the children of God."

Jesus was teaching his disciples on a mountainside. A multitude of people were listening. The truths He spoke on that occasion are recorded in Matthew 5. The whole account (Matthew 5:1 to 8:1) has since been termed "The Sermon on the Mount." Within this "sermon" are nine texts often lovingly referred to as The Beatitudes. Each one begins, "Blessed are . . ." I would commend to you a careful study and memorization of each text. For our purposes in this letter, let me share my experience with just one of them.

Whenever I hear the text, "Blessed are the peacemakers, . . ." it seems to me that something has been left out. To me the text starts, "Girls, Girls! Blessed are the peacemakers. . . ." You see, I have a sister just older than I. To this day we are not only sisters but very good friends. Nevertheless, during our childhood we had our sibling disagreements. Sometimes in the heat of an especially boisterous quarrel our mother would interfere with, "Girls, Girls! Blessed are the *peacemakers*, . . ." and then with special emphasis she would add, "for *they* shall be called the children of God."

I don't know that I ever really comprehended what a peacemaker was. Nor am I sure that in the middle of those childish conflicts I really wanted much understanding. However, of recent years I've begun to learn that a peacemaker is not necessarily one who gives in to be walked on. Rather, he recognizes needs in himself and in others and seeks to understand from every reference point. He strives to listen—really listen. He seeks to separate ideas from people and never to reject the person. These are some of the insights I've been gaining. I like to talk about them and get ideas from other people. And, would you believe, one of the persons I enjoy input from the most is none other than my sister!

John 13:34, 35. "A new commandment I give unto you, That ye love one another; as I have loved you, that ye also love one another. By this shall all men know that ye are my disciples, if ye have love one to another."

In this discussion with His disciples, Jesus must not have replaced the commandments given directly to Moses on Mount Sinai, for later in that same conversation He referred to keeping His commandments (plural). Nevertheless, He was certainly emphasizing the need to love our fellow Christians.

How do you love on command? That puzzled me for a long time. Then, one day as I sat devoutly in my church seat (it was not a pew, because the church was being remodeled, and we were meeting in the gymnasium) I found myself in a very critical attitude. In my mind I would categorize each person who came by. One lady was pious because she wore that funny hat—she must be ultraconservative (and hats weren't even in vogue). Another lady, looking like the latest fashion plate, must certainly be "uppity." Oh, my, I'm almost too ashamed to admit these awful judgments. But they were there, and they were real.

Praise God for sending the Holy Spirit to bring my thinking up short. How, with that kind of an attitude, could I possibly love anyone? And then I tried an experiment. As I watched individuals come into the service I would mentally say, "I'm glad you're here today. God loves you. It may have been a struggle to come today, but I'll pray that you receive a blessing." Would you believe, my attitude changed? I found myself actually loving persons I had never met—persons whom, only moments before, I had criticized and mentally rebuked. If you want an interesting experience sometime, try it out.

Jeremiah 32:17. "Ah Lord God! behold, thou hast made the heaven and the earth by thy great power and stretched out arm, and there is nothing too hard for thee."

Jeremiah's statement recently captured my attention, and I am in the process of incorporating it into my life right now. As I try to visualize its meaning, I immediately think of a situation that occurred just a few weeks ago.

I had made arrangements with the hospital to provide learning experiences for the students. All seemed to go well until the nursing administrators made some decisions that could adversely affect the students' program of learning. The administrators were reasonable people, but I felt they did not have adequate information on which to base their judgments. Somehow, without seeming impudent, I needed to get them to reconsider their decision.

I prayed about the matter. Even in the stillness of the night I was awake, talking it over with the Lord. The next morning I met with a representative of the group. We had barely started our conversation when she reached for pencil and paper. "How would you like it to be?" she asked. And she proceeded to write out a directive that considered the students' needs.

I was surprised. Within fifteen minutes the problem was solved. "But that was too easy," I thought. And then the counterthought, "Lord, God . . . there is nothing too hard for thee."

John 10:14-28. "I am the good shepherd, and know my sheep, and am known of mine. . . . My sheep hear my voice, and I know them, and they follow me: and I give unto them eternal life; and they shall never perish, neither shall any man pluck them out of my hand."

The director of clinical ministries (chaplain's department) and the director of nursing service were talking about employing a nurse in a liaison role to help hospital staff meet the spiritual needs of patients. They had talked with me about filling that position. At first I felt elated about the possibilities. But as the seriousness of the responsibility began to sink into my realization, I became awestricken.

While I went from unit to unit supervising the nursing students (this happened while you were a student, Georgia) I was carefully contemplating my decisions. One day as I left the hospital and started to drive home, the calling weighed heavily on my mind. Just before I got to the freeway entrance, I passed a field where a shepherd was herding a flock of sheep. In one glance I noted a small lamb stumbling over some of the rough clods in the field. "I feel just as helpless as that little lamb," I thought to myself. I was gaining speed to pull into the flow of freeway traffic. I looked in the mirror and flipped the blinker light. "But I have a Good Shepherd. I have nothing to fear." I entered the freeway and thanked God for all His promises.

John 14:1-3. "Let not your heart be troubled: ye believe in God, believe also in me. In my Father's house are many mansions: if it were not so, I would have told you. I go to prepare a place for you. And if I go and prepare a place for you, I will come again, and receive you unto myself; that where I am, there ye may be also."

Georgia, this is the day we are looking for. Sometimes I feel like saying, "Jesus, I'll be so glad when You come. I want to see You. I want to visit with You." And I suspect you have those same feelings.

I want very much to be the person God wants me to be. I know that you do, too. He has given us the guidelines in the form of the Holy Scriptures. He sent His Son to demonstrate and give us the pattern. He sends the Holy Spirit to guide our pathways.

And one glorious day He will gather His faithful children. I want to be there, and I know you do, too.

May God bless you as you go out from this school to practice your profession. I'll be praying for you. I need your prayers, too. And finally, when all is said and done, I'll meet you in the mansions above.

Love,
Beulah

And, dear reader, whoever you are, wherever you are, God loves you, too. He wants you in heaven with Him. I'm looking forward to meeting you and to introducing you to Georgia.